NIJINSKY

Le Carnaval

THE ART OF
NIJINSKY

BY GEOFFREY WHITWORTH
WITH TEN ILLUSTRATIONS BY
DOROTHY MULLOCK

BENJAMIN BLOM, INC.
Publishers New York 1972

First published London, 1913
Reissued 1972 by
Benjamin Blom, Inc.
New York, N. Y. 10025

Library of Congress
Catalog Card Number 72-83753

Printed in the
United States of America

NOTE

THIS little book owes a great deal to the assistance of M. Nijinsky, who himself gave every facility, both on and off the stage, for its preparation. Artist and Author wish to record their thanks to M. Nijinsky for his kindness.

CONTENTS

ILLUSTRATIONS

NIJINSKY

CHAPTER I

INTRODUCTION

THE last edition of the *Encyclopædia Britannica*, published in 1910, contains an excellent little essay on the Ballet, which ends, after bewailing the modern degeneracy of the art, with these ill-omened words:

"It seems unlikely that we shall see any revival of the best period and style of dancing until a higher standard of grace and manners becomes fashionable in society. Only in an atmosphere of ceremony, courtesy, and chivalry can the dance maintain itself in perfection."

Well, it is a dangerous thing to be a

prophet ; and that this particular prophet has proved most happily at fault will be plain to everyone. The passage is quoted here, however, not at all for the simple pleasure of refuting it, but rather because it aptly indicates some of those more than ordinary difficulties which lie in wait for any English critic of the Russian Ballet. For it must be remembered that our author of the *Encyclopædia* was hardly, if at all, behind the times in which he wrote. M. Diaghilew's company did not make its first appearance in London till the summer of 1911, and though before then there had been considerable evidence of a revival in individual dancing, concerted dancing on a definite theme (which we may take as a practical definition of the ballet) had seldom reached a lower stage of insignificance. In those days,

INTRODUCTION

few even of the best informed among the
critics were aware of what was going on
in Russia, and it is scarcely strange that
London's first experience of the Russian
Ballet took the majority of us utterly by
surprise.

During the last few years a mighty
revolution has had to be worked in our
ideas concerning the whole art of the
dance. And this not only as regards the
dances of the ballroom. In the theatre
the change has been no less striking, and
we have found ourselves in the position
of being forced to develop a completely
fresh set of æsthetic standards so as to
keep pace with the development of a
tradition which for us, previously, had
been little more than a dead and obsolete
form. In this task we have been obliged
to proceed mainly by the light of nature.
There have been few to guide us, and

for once the critics, both amateur and professional, have found themselves in the same galley.

I know, of course, that in the interval which separates us from the date, say, of that article in the *Encyclopædia*, a good deal has been written on the subject of the ballet and its revival. We have had, for instance, Mr. Crawford Flitch's able volume on *Modern Dancing and Dancers*, to which I hereby declare a conspicuous and inevitable debt. But not so far, perhaps, has the subject found a really adequate treatment,[1] and, in the absence of such treatment, all hasty conclusions will be wise to acknowledge the limits within which they have been arrived at.

[1] I refer only to English books. But mention must be made of the expert and sumptuous volume by the Russian critic, Svétlow, which may now be obtained in the French version of M. Calvocoressi under the title of *Le Ballet Contemporain*.

INTRODUCTION

As for the present book, it can make no claim whatever to provide a detailed and reasoned account of the Russian Ballet, or yet of the great artist and dancer whose name is its ornament. Its character will be that of a purely personal impression, supported, I hope, by some wider considerations, but still essentially an impression, and with the value of an impression rather than of a work of studied criticism.

In spite of obvious shortcomings, there is something to be said for such a method. For dancing is one of those arts which least repay too dry an exposition. In this it is like music, and most unlike the monumental arts of sculpture, painting, literature, which, in virtue of their very persistence, have the less claim to be recorded. For we can read the book, or see the picture for ourselves, and go to

criticism for information or sound judgment rather than for a verbal *réchauffée* of
an accessible and authentic charm. But
in an art which perishes, the mere impression of an observer, however inade-
quate, may be of value. The written
word survives ; so that a Vestris dances
again in the most fatuous praise of his
contemporaries, while even that famous
picture in prose by Walter Pater ac-
quires a fresh and thrilling meaning
since " Mona Lisa " has vanished from
the Louvre.

The aim of this essay, then, is, first and
foremost, to preserve an impression. As
to its manner, I need only forestall, if it
may be, one possible objection. " You
call your book," someone might say, "*The
Art of Nijinsky*. Very well. But there
are pages and pages occupied with quite
extraneous things. . . . We thought to find

the appreciation of an artistic personality, and you give us irrelevant views on the art of the ballet as a whole ! "

The fact is, of course, that it would be absurd to attempt the appreciation of an art like Nijinsky's by any method that excluded some treatment, at least, of the medium in which that art displays itself. This is true, certainly, of the art of every dancer, but in the present case especially so ; if only because Nijinsky has chosen to throw in his lot with that movement in the modern theatre which is antagonistic to anything like an undue emphasis on the talent of the individual.

That the whole is greater than the part is a hard precept for mime or dancer who happens to be blessed with personality. The temptation to dominate is strong. But he who will accept and act upon this principle is sure of his reward; for so he will participate in a greatness that is greater even than his own—the supreme greatness of an impersonal work of art. Now, it is a chief glory of the Russian Ballet that it has not only afforded a perfect medium of expression to one of the most outstanding geniuses of the modern stage, but that it has also found in that genius an aptitude for subordination which is among the rarest and finest virtues an artist of the theatre can possess.

It is for this reason that our treatment of the art of Nijinsky must needs go further than a consideration of its purely individual aspect. To do less would be unjust to various factors which contribute to the central effect. It would also be unjust to Nijinsky himself, whose method shows such a perfect sense of the action and interaction of elements as complex as they are mutually dependent.

CHAPTER II

THE CAREER OF NIJINSKY

WASLAW NIJINSKY is a native of Warsaw. He was born some twenty-three years ago, the son of parents who were both closely connected with the branch of the Russian Imperial Ballet established in that city. His mother was a dancer. Likewise his father, who was early promoted to the rank of ballet-master, and took an honourable part in the development of a national school of dancing as opposed to the Italian school whose influence in Warsaw had previously been supreme. The young Nijinsky soon began to manifest the characteristics of genius, and at nine years of age he was transferred from

Warsaw and enlisted as a scholar in the college of the Imperial Ballet at St. Petersburg.

A correspondent of the *Manchester Guardian* has given a neat *précis* of that famous system to which is owing so much of the supremacy of the Russian Imperial Ballet. " To-day," he writes, " the ballet is a vast State organisation with an annual budget of over a million roubles. The members of the ballet troups are Government servants, with the attendant rights and privileges of this class. Most of the *corps du ballet* are of quite humble origin, and are generally the daughters of small clerks, of the theatre attendants, who have naturally numerous facilities for advancing their children, and of former ballet-dancers. The training of a dancer is long and severe. After having passed through a process of selection and of physical inspection, girls are taken into the Government ballet schools from the age of eight to ten. At school they remain, on an average, about seven years. Then, after passing the final examination, they are enrolled as members of the *corps du ballet*. The step from corps dancer to première danseuse depends entirely on the dancer's own ability and talent. Sometimes, as in the case of Anna Pavlova "—and, he might have added, of Nijinsky—" promotion comes almost immediately, and usually it is easy to recognise the future ballerina before she has reached her twentieth year. Practice, however, is essential, and even to the end of her career the most talented ballerina must practise three or four hours a day."

Such is the course of training which in recent years has produced more than one dancing star of the first magnitude—a training whose principles are bound up with a tradition of art unequalled for strength and self-consistency. Never, indeed, has genius been more happy in its education than Nijinsky's. Never has it come upon the scene at a moment more opportune for its fruition. Only the very briefest résumé of the history of the ballet in Russia will be enough to make this clear.

Just as the beginnings of the modern literary movement in Russia are traceable, through Pouchkine, to the European and particularly to the French culture of the eighteenth century, so the art of the dance was originally borrowed by Russia from Italy, its first authentic home. Russian Ballet, then, is essentially one with a main trend of European expression, and, although certainly modified by the national character, is, by its very antecedents, perfectly fitted to take its place among the arts of a cosmopolitan as distinct from a merely native art.

The love of dancing is no doubt spontaneous among the Russian peasantry, and always has been. But the development of this natural impulse into art dates, for all practical purposes, from the patronage of the Empress Anna Ivanovna, who, in the year 1735, appointed a Neapolitan composer and a French ballet-master to preside over her newly instituted Dramatic School. Catherine II worthily carried on the work. A second theatre was established in Moscow, and the whole organisation was placed on a firm basis of relation with the bureaucratic régime. Throughout the eighteenth century the Russian Imperial Ballet must have maintained and, little by little, strengthened its position ; although it was France, with dancers like Noverre and the great immi-

grant family of Vestris, that took unques-
tionably the lead. The Russian traveller
and romantic, Karamzine, has actually
recorded his impression of French dancing
as he saw it in Paris in 1790, and later on
in the same year at Lyon. "There is no
one like Vestris!" he ejaculates, and leaves
us in no possible doubt that he had never
witnessed anything half so wonderful in
the theatres of his own country.

Not, indeed, until well on in the
nineteenth century did the Imperial
Ballet at St. Petersburg begin to compete
at all seriously with the art as practised
in Paris or in Milan. But then advance
was rapid, though the principal performers were still largely imported from
Italy and the ballet-masters from France.
Nor is it until the middle of the century that we come to a period of distinc-
tively Russian control, with the advent of

the first native director of real eminence, that Marius Petipa, to whose work in the 'fifties and 'sixties so much of the present supremacy of the Russian Ballet is undoubtedly due. The ballets produced by Petipa still conformed to the traditional type—three or four acts, and lasting a whole evening. But Petipa did work of enormous importance by assisting the emergence of a national feeling and by encouraging native talent to take its place in the highest grades of the ballet.

It was under his rule, at any rate, that Russian dancing began to achieve self-sufficiency, and to realise itself as equal, nay, superior, to the dancing of any other country in Europe.

Heir to this period of artistic expansiveness, Nijinsky began his career as a student in the Imperial School. A little senior to him was a whole galaxy of genius, which included such famous names as those of Mme. Karsarvina, Anna Pavlova, Mordkin, and Adolf Bolm. The scene was already crowded ; but by his eighteenth year Nijinsky had successfully asserted his claim to a place beside these others in the very front rank of Russian dancers. And this rapidity of advancement was not due simply to the fact that Nijinsky could leap into the air a little higher than any of his fellow-students, nor yet that he was more proficient than all of them in the time-honoured tricks of *entrechat* and *pirouette*. From the first there had been evident in his dancing that promise of genius which no technical skill can simulate, but which through technical skill alone can blossom into its finest flower.

Now, in addition to the growing fame of Nijinsky, the first decade of the present century witnessed the rise of several novel

Le Spectre de la Rose

tendencies which were all of obvious and capital importance in the development of the art of the ballet. New artistic impulses were coming to life all over Europe, and most of them had a definite relation with the art of the theatre in one or other of its numerous forms. The full history of these fresh developments, and of the resulting cleavage between the old ballet and the new, has yet to be written. Here we must be content to trace that cleavage in part to the influence of a new school of music which had risen to power within Russia itself, in part also to the more extraneous influences which came, via Moscow, from Prof. Reinhardt the German, and from Gordon Craig the Englishman. Nor must we forget the liberating force which sprang from the art of Isadora Duncan, whose heroic practice has done far more than any precept of philosophy to widen our ideas as to the intellectual and spiritual possibilities of the dance.

Such were a few of the influences which all appeared to be steadily converging upon the city of St. Petersburg. That something a little startling was bound to happen seemed certain. For on the one hand, you had the unique instrument of the Russian Ballet, an instrument quietly perfected through centuries of care and accumulating tradition ; on the other hand, a whole new range of ideas and feelings, only waiting, it seemed, for a spark, to flame up into a new and wonderful life. Something however still was wanting—a *tertium quid* —and this was found presently in the person of M. Serge de Diaghilew.

It was in 1908 that M. Diaghilew first turned his attention to the Russian Ballet. Previously he had been engaged in producing Russian Opera—the master-pieces of Moussorgsky, Rimsky-Korsakov, etc.—outside Russia itself and in a manner before undreamed of, save perhaps in the Imperial opera-houses of St. Petersburg and Moscow. He now conceived the idea that there was a future also for Russian Ballet, if only it could be produced at all adequately in the trying circumstances of a European tour. The difficulties in organising such a scheme were vast, and they were difficulties insurmountable by an artist pure and simple. But M. Diaghilew, above all things, is a business man, and before very long he was successful in arranging his great plan of a limited series of productions in Rome, Paris, Berlin, and finally England, with a company drawn from regular performers at the Imperial theatres, and including some of the finest dancers of

the Imperial Ballet. Several entirely
new ballets were soon added to the existing repertoire, and from the start a
definite note of modernity was sounded
which proclaimed the Diaghilew ballet
as an exponent of the new revolution in
the art of the dance. In accordance with
this purpose the services of the most
advanced producers and designers were
secured—men like Michel Fokine, Benois,
and Léon Bakst. While at the same
time, with the instinct of a born im-
pressario, M. Diaghilew also acquired the
services of the young Nijinsky, at that time
in the first hey-day of success at the
Imperial Ballet. M. Diaghilew must
have speedily realised that if he could
only retain the exclusive services of the
wonderful young dancer, he would also
have gone far towards making his organisation a permanent one and altogether

safe from the possibility of awkward competition. In a sense, indeed, Nijinsky was the key to the position.

From his own standpoint, on the other hand, Nijinsky himself was scarcely less clear-sighted in his view of the trend of affairs. The conservatism of the Imperial Ballet was becoming a byword among the more advanced spirits of the period, and having once tasted the joyous freedom of service with M. Diaghilew, he was not likely to remain content with the rules and regulations of an organisation which, in his view, was lamentably incapable of marching with the times. The result was that after one or two excursions with the Diaghilew ballet, Nijinsky's relations with the Imperialists became awkwardly strained. In the early part of 1911 the strain became intolerable, and on an unimportant pretext of costume

Nijinsky received, and accepted, his dismissal at the hands of the Imperial authorities.

From that time onwards Nijinsky has thrown himself heart and soul into the new enterprise. As the leading male dancer in M. Diaghilew's ballet, he has naturally been obliged to undertake rôles of every kind ; but it would be hard to say in which of them all he has been most admired. There is a wide gulf between the sweet conventional charm of Armide's slave and the austere and subtle beauty of the Faune ; but Nijinsky's art is as many-sided as a circle, and though no doubt he allows himself the luxury of having favourites, a mere spectator could scarcely guess which of all his many rôles he liked the best.

During the last year or so the career of Nijinsky has developed suddenly in a new, but not altogether unforeseen, direction. He has enlarged his sphere of activity beyond the actual boards of the theatre, and has, in some sense, assumed the mantle of M. Fokine, who had previously been responsible for the choreographic arrangement of most of the ballets. Already Nijinsky has designed the dancing of three new ballets : the *Prélude à l'Après-Midi d'un Faune*, *Jeux*, and *Le Sacre du Printemps ;* and in so doing has taken definitely his place among the great master-ballet-dancers of history.

CHAPTER III

As we saw in the last chapter, Nijinsky's technique is the result of a system of training which, however superior, is similar in kind to that found in several other European schools of ballet dancing. We know how high a standard of skill may be attained by almost anyone with an aptitude for dancing if trained on these lines. Indeed there are several dancers in M. Diaghilew's company, and we have seen others at various times and places, whom one would not hesitate to put in the very foremost rank. But about Nijinsky's dancing there is something altogether unique—an exotic quality

24

which cannot be measured or referred
to any standard of purely technical excellence. The word Genius, I believe,
is rather out of fashion just now ; but
it has been used once or twice already
in the course of this little book, and now
it must be used again, if only because
there is really no other word which at
all expresses that peculiar element in
Nijinsky's art which has here, somehow
or other, to be explored.

Now, one of the principal marks of
genius is the combination in one and the
same person of talents, common enough
in themselves, but rarely found together.
Nijinsky's art is full of such combinations.
One of them, for example, is that union
of strength with lightness which is, perhaps, the most obvious feature of his style.
Apart from the muscular development of
hip and thigh, Nijinsky gives one the

impression of being very slight in build. His body is slim as a boy's. His arms are delicate. His wrists and ankles almost dainty. While watching him dance it may not seem strange that a being so agile should be able to lift and hold, a hair's-breadth from the ground, another being like unto himself but frailer even than he—one of those Sylphides, perhaps, that sway like river-reeds in the breeze or hover like thistledown. Yet, thinking it over, you have to realise that after all it was a grown woman he held there, and that only the apparent ease with which he held her cheated you into the belief that she was light as air. Try for yourself a similar feat, and you will know how much of physical strength is needed to perform it even clumsily. And Nijinsky is nothing if not graceful. And graceful strength is strength twice over.

Les Sylphides

HIS ART

Another fusion of qualities most noticeable in the art of Nijinsky, and most rare, is that fusion of utter freedom of movement with unfailing sense for decorative effect. Freedom of movement can be attained, no doubt, by practice. And a good " producer " may contrive that the main attitudes of a dance shall be correct in themselves and sufficiently beautiful. But with Nijinsky, pose, attitude, seems to be an instinct rather than a lesson learnt, and even in the wildest orgy of motion his feeling for outline never fails. At any given moment his silhouette, could one descry it, would be found, I believe, to form a lovely pattern. And not by any means is this a question of mere training, as may be proved by comparing Nijinsky's style with that of the other most competent dancers in the same company.

NIJINSKY

It must be, I think, this sense of outline which also endows Nijinsky's art with that exquisite neatness which some have actually interpreted as its limitation. Dancing, such people say, is of the essence of freedom. To restrain is to sterilise and to reduce the living body of man to nothing better than a mechanism of springs and steel. Well, there is this amount of truth in such a criticism : that Nijinsky's method does not actually seem so nicely adapted to express certain moods of natural abandonment as, say, Mordkin expressed in that famous Bacchanale he danced with Anna Pavlova. Still, no artist is at his best in every mood, and to expect him to be so is to deny to him the gift of personality. As a matter of fact, a feeling for outline like Nijinsky's allows a far wider range of effect than that possible to a looser method ; implies, too, the possession of a far surer and subtler intellectual faculty. "The great and golden rule of art . . .," said Blake, "is this : that the more distinct, sharp, and wiry the bounding line, the more perfect the work of art. The want of this determinate and bounding form evidences the idea of want in the artist's mind."

Certainly there is no such void in the mind of Nijinsky. His mental vigour is as keen as his physical ; and, richly endowed as he is with every perfection of technique, he is still the unerring master of his material, never its slave.

This brings us to the last item in our little catalogue of combined qualities—an item which can be easily expressed by saying that Nijinsky is not only a great dancer, but also a great actor. An opinion, this, which differs radically from that of so high an authority as Miss Ellen Terry, whose gaily intuitive essay on the Russian Ballet was so strangely cool in its appreciation of the dramatic side of Nijinsky's art. In the next chapter, however, I shall be giving some brief notes on the chief ballets in which Nijinsky takes part, which, if nothing else, cannot fail to emphasize the variety and the vividness of mood and atmosphere evoked. Several of the rôles are of a conventional and even abstract type, but even these Nijinsky has individualised to an extraordinary degree. And how else, one may well ask, can this be done, except by the force of a powerful histrionic imagination—or, at any rate, of something so nearly akin to that faculty as to be scarcely distinguishable from it ?

Nijinsky's art, after all, is primarily imaginative. Dancing with him is an expression of mood, not of mere grace or rhythm. Even in the purely graceful ballets like *Les Sylphides* or *Le Pavillon d'Armide*, he shows us a mind at work creating gracefulness rather than a mere body being graceful. It is difficult enough to analyse, but one feels that all this splendid and apparently inspired resourcefulness must be bound up, somehow, with Nijinsky's own personal attitude towards life itself.

A man, of course, may be an excellent dancer, and at the same time only very moderate in his interest in or understanding of life as a whole. Such a negative attitude, however, will show itself at once in the quality of art resulting. That quality may be coldly beautiful, or hotly sensuous, or merely pretty. But its intellectual appeal will be nil. Nijinsky's dancing, on the contrary, is a thing as much of head and soul as of

31

heart and body, and claims the rapt attention of all our faculties for its understanding.

To meet Nijinsky in private life is to gain a perfect confirmation of any belief you may hold as to the presence in such a great artist of intellectual power. At a first introduction you might experience, perhaps, a shade of disappointment. A far cry, it seems, from the glamour of a great theatre to the sudden seclusion of a London drawing-room. And this quiet little gentleman in immaculate English clothes, can it—can it really be Nijinsky? He is not tall enough, surely—and his hair looks so sleek and dark and normal. Not till later on, when you have had time to notice the fine and subtle modelling of the cheek, the narrow, flickering eyes, the clean but rounded lips, will you begin to realise that this must be he. And after a while, when the first hesitation of his manner gives way to vivacity, when the whole face brightens with the thought that is a little difficult to express in a foreign tongue, then at last you come to know that all is indeed well. For here is a man who is intensely, sincerely, nervously alive. He has a brain—there is no doubt of it. And you feel you would like to know what he thinks about everything.

CHAPTER IV

THE BALLETS

AT the end of the book will be found a complete list of the ballets performed in England in which Nijinsky himself has taken part. Here we deal, rather more fully, with nine typical ballets, being those which Miss Dorothy Mullock has chosen as subjects for her pictures.

LE LAC DES CYGNES

This ballet may be fitly taken first and by way of introduction to those which follow, since it stands rather by itself— neither definitely dramatic nor merely illustrative of its musical accompaniment. In spirit it belongs to that older kind of

34

Le Lac des Cygnes

ballet which, though nominally inspired by history or legend, is largely independent of both, and prone at any moment to drift from the central theme, and to spend itself on interminable embroideries devoid of action.

The Swans of the Swan lake were enchanted birds who danced, in the form of white maidens, by moonlight at the water's edge. A young prince of the realm is hunting by the lake, and half in jest, half in earnest, pursues and takes captive the queen of the Swan-maidens. He woos her, but she escapes and flies off to the lake again, leaving him to go home again disconsolate. There presently, in the palace of his fathers, it is the day of the young prince's betrothal. Great celebrations are being held. A splendid company is assembled, and they perform pompous and brilliant dances. The prince

dances too, more brilliantly than them all.
But still he is sick at heart, distracted by
the thought of the Swan-queen. For a
beauteous stranger has been introduced,
and seeing her he experiences a second
time that fond and desperate longing he
had felt by the side of the Swan lake.
At length he brings himself to dance with
the strange lady. New life courses through
his veins. He is spurred on to greater
and greater feats, to more and more impossible figures. He leaps high in the
air, and the company stands amazed.
This is not dancing, they whisper, but
black magic. Magic indeed. . . . For
suddenly, in a thunderous spell of dark-
ness, the strange lady, the Swan-queen,
disappears ; and the last tableau shows us
the shore of the lake again, and the young
prince, hot in pursuit, but by an inch too
late. . . . For there is nothing now but

a flock of white swans, vanishing over the water.

Nijinsky, of course, impersonates the prince—the slim and debonair young prince of the fairy tale. In the first scene of eager reconnaissance, and in the final tragic tableau by the water-side, we have his genius for pantomime splendidly exhibited. While, in the middle scene— the dance and courtly festival—he demonstrates the full resources of his virtuosity, performing the rarest and most difficult figures with the ease that can belong to no one but the born technician. In some other ballets Nijinsky's style becomes so free and unconventional that one is tempted to forget the years of study out of which it has evolved. But his supremacy in this ballet of *Le Lac des Cygnes* is perfect proof, if such be needed, that Nijinsky has undergone and mastered every phase of training in the most orthodox and traditional modes of his art.

To-day *Le Lac des Cygnes* survives alone in the Diaghilew repertoire to indicate what Russian ballet was like in the days of the great Petipa. For the choreography and the general arrangement of the dances are in the tradition of that master, and the music is Tschaikovsky's—quite " the latest thing," no doubt, at the time when the ballet was first produced. To some of us now it may all seem a trifle old-fashioned ; but those who are interested to see the art of dancing in its pure and classic form, could wish for no more typical display. *Le Lac des Cygnes* triumphantly succeeds in being what it sets out to be, and it would be a thousand pities if later and more exotic flavours were to dull our palate for such wholesome and, withal, such magnificent fare.

THE BALLETS

One of the earlier productions of M. Fokine, *Armide*, forms an important link with such traditional ballets as *Le Lac des Cygnes* and the other productions of Petipa.

As originally produced it included a prologue and an epilogue, with so much genuine plot in them as to supply the action of the ballet with an interesting *raison d'être*. There was the old story of the tired traveller and the insinuating stranger, and the grateful offer of a lodging for the night. And then, after the dream, which was the ballet, the scene of awakening and sinister disillusion. As recently performed, however, this pantomime setting has been clipped away, with the result that certain episodes in the ballet have lost something of their point.

39

But the natural quality of the thing is untouched, and *Armide* still remains perhaps the most complete, as it is certainly the most luxuriant, example of conventional ballet-dancing which the Russians have shown us.

There are marvellous moments all through. One of them comes when Nijinsky makes his first and curiously modest entry into that wonderful scene of pink and green and blue, that scene which reminds one, in its luscious colouring, of all the beautiful good things to eat in the world. Truly, the effect would be sugary if it were not so cool, strident if not so infinitely modulated ; and if there be some who have actually found it so, I can only answer that they have not seen it through my eyes. As to Nijinsky himself, there can hardly be two opinions. His presentment of Armide's

Le Pavillon d Armide

familiar slave is one of a dozen master-
pieces. Not only does he find and use
the opportunity of displaying some of
the most intricate and characteristic steps
of the Russian method, but he also endows
the whole spectacle with just that appropriate tensity of feeling which alone can
raise fine dancing to the plane of fine
art. For Nijinsky, the vivid, radiant
boy, is also the hierophant of mysteries,
and in the glamour of his presence *Armide*
comes to seem not merely a matchless
display of lovely form in lovely motion,
but also a type of the supreme functioning
of a state of being most strange and
utterly alien from our own.

The court of Armide, one believes, is
part of a definite and settled polity, with
its own laws, its own customs, and its
own business from day to day. It is
more objective in feeling than the scene

of any other of the Russian ballets—less
a dream than a vision, so that when it
comes to an end we feel that it is ourselves that are losing touch with reality
rather than that what appeared as reality
is now proving itself an illusion.

The secret of this effect is twofold.
Partly it lies in the exquisite purity of
convention which the ballet retains
throughout, partly in the conviction of
aloofness which Nijinsky brings to his
rendering of the part of Armide's slave.
He never forgets for a moment where
and what he is, and though, as we have
hinted, *Armide* is first and foremost a
choreographic ballet, Nijinsky has also
made of it a splendid occasion for the
practice of his faculty for imaginative
characterisation.

This, I think, explains the fact that
one can return to the *Pavillon d'Armide*

time after time, and with a sense of never-failing refreshment. For the art of Nijinsky has made one free of a strange country, where dancing and simple melodies of music are the natural language of the soul, the perfect expression of an essential and peculiar joy.

LE CARNAVAL

" Music," said Noverre, " is to dancing what words are to music—a simile which means nothing except that dance music is, or ought to be, the written poem which determines the movements and the action of the dancer." And truly the artist of the ballet has always been in debt to the musician, while there have been countless efforts actually to interpret musical compositions through the medium of the dance. In no instance, however—so far, at least, as I am aware—has the effort been so elaborate and at the same time so successful as in this ballet of M. Fokine's, set to the music of Schumann. For though we find in *Les Sylphides* a parallel attempt to visualise music, scarcely there does the music hold its own with the stage picture, and it is only now and then that the fusion between action and music becomes complete. In *Carnaval* the fusion is complete all through.

The reason is, probably, that though *Le Carnaval* was written with no earthly idea as to its suitability for the framework of a ballet, yet theme by theme the composer had in his mind's eye definite images which were intrinsically of such a kind as could be well expressed in terms of pantomime.

Le Carnaval is a work of Schumann's early years, and in these " Scènes Mignonnes,"as he described them,there is expressed all the gay and witty self-consciousness of a quite young man. The ideas at the back of this music are not, then, purely musical ones, but the various themes are expressive of a company of fantastic figures, all well-known personages translated into a private world of whimsy which Schumann had constructed for his own amusement and convenience. Here were a set of characters ready made for the ballet—Florestan and Eusebius (the one representing a stormy, the other a dreamy side of Schumann's temperament), Pierrot, Harlequin, Papillon, Columbine, Chiarina, and the rest—the most adorable collection of puppets, tender, grave and gay, that have ever been gathered together on a stage.

The method of the ballet's action is simple enough. The music is left to tell the story, and, punctual to the commencement of every theme, the appropriate character comes flitting on to the stage, to dance its little *pas* and then flit off again to make way for the next. The stage setting is as empty and dignified as a musical stave, and the little figures hurry across it, singly or in groups, almost like musical notation come to life and colour. This means that the music is never strained for a moment to carry action of a greater concrete significance than itself; and we can both hear and see at the same moment, with no troublesome endeavour to combine or distinguish our sensations.

Nijinsky's Harlequin is, of course, an unforgettable figure : not at all the blustering, magnificent Harlequin of Italian comedy, but a sly fellow, slickly insinuating, naughtily intimate. He is always whispering subtle secrets to Columbine, and is saved from viciousness only by his

Le Carnaval

unerring sense of fun. Certainly he is the most uncanny and the least human of all Nijinsky's creations. For this Harlequin is the very soul of mischief—half Puck— but Puck with a sting, and with a body like a wire of tempered steel.

LE SPECTRE DE LA ROSE

Open your eyes that close
To this maiden dream so light ;
I am the wraith of a rose
You wore at the dance last night.
You gathered me pearly and wet
With the silver tears of the dew ;
In that glittering throng I let
You carry me all night through.

You were my death, you know,
But you cannot keep away
My rosy spirit ; to and fro
It shall dance by your bed till day.
Be not afraid—I ask no dole
Of pity or prayers or sighs ;
This scented sweetness is my soul,
And it comes from Paradise.

NIJINSKY

Envy, rather, my fate :
For many would die to rest,
So pure and so consecrate,
In the tender tomb of your breast—
On its marble front to repose
Where a poet's kiss for me
Has written : Here lies a rose
Where a king might give all to be !

Thus one might render very roughly into English those verses of Théophile Gautier which have suggested this beautiful little ballet of *Le Spectre de la Rose*. And here it is just worth noting that Gautier's poem was written in the year 1837, and that the ballet, as we see it to-day, seems to distil the very finest essence of that particular quality of sentiment which we call Early Victorian.

But more than this, *Le Spectre de la Rose* is a vision of youth—*la Jeunesse*—not wild, passionate, but virgin youth, just learning to be troubled with its first wonderful dream. Only in an atmosphere

48

of some moral severity, one feels, could this natural impulse achieve so chaste and at the same time so fervent an awakening. And one rightly knows that love, with this young girl come back from the ball to her little white and blue bedroom, is something that she would never dare to discuss, scarce even think of, but only feel, now and again, in a little trembling gust of sensibility. All this and more, far more, has Mme. Karsavina conveyed in her unequalled performance. And Nijinsky . . .

He truly shows us the very heart of a red rose. For so quiet and tender is his dancing, so exquisitely adapted to the theme, that he becomes the very being he would portray, a spirit rather than a man, a fairy thing and as light as a waft of perfume.

Technically, *Le Spectre de la Rose* is

D

most interesting for the delicate economy
of the means employed.   Notice also that
the personalities of the dancers are but
slightly insisted on, and that the agree-
ment between them is conceived as being
so perfect that one is frequently aware of
little more than the rhythm in which
both are fused.   The steps of the dance,
too, are appropriately simple, like the
scenery, and like the music of Weber's
delicious " Invitation."

LES SYLPHIDES

A friend of mine, returning home
from a performance of *Les Sylphides*, sat
down while the memory of what he
had seen was still fresh, to record if he
could the varied evolutions of the ballet
in a series of algebraical symbols.   He
told me that he was astonished at the
intricate beauty of the resulting ratios,

and boasted that a perusal of his page of formulæ gave him a pleasure that was almost as great as that which he had experienced while sitting at ease in his seat at Covent Garden. Personally, I would not care to make a similar experiment ; yet I do recognise in dancing of a certain kind just that perfectness of symmetry which, it may be, can most fitly be translated into the medium of mathematics, and for which in words, at any rate, can be found no possible equivalent.

In a figure more natural to one's own mode of thought, let me describe *Les Sylphides* as a spiritual ballet—a ballet, that is to say, which insists very little on qualities of human flesh and blood but demands the exercise of mind, soul, spirit, or whatever principle you will that is furthest removed from the appetites of sense. For certainly the beauty of *Les Sylphides* has little to do with the body, and in this respect partakes essentially of the nature of music, although as an actual visualisation of music (in the sense that *Carnaval* is such) it cannot be taken so very seriously. The less one thinks about Chopin, in fact, the more will one enjoy *Les Sylphides*. For Chopin's is the music of the velvet warmth of summer nights, and there is something sweet and scented in the air that is the breath of his dim, romantic world. But the country of *Les Sylphides* is cold and clear and fragile, a land of frozen moonlight, which, if you tried to reach it, would shimmer out into a thousand spangles at the first touch of your finger-tips.

As a ballet *Les Sylphides* is perfectly simple, perfectly refined. The long, deep-waisted skirts of the dancers are substantially the same as those worn in the middle of the last century by Grisi, Fanny Elssler, or Taglioni. And there is nothing esoteric in the dancing ; only the genius of a pure tradition, perfected and conserved. Nijinsky, of course, in his rich, black surcoat, stands out very prominent among the white ranks of the sylphides whom it is his happy task to shepherd. His dancing, too, is as completely true to the orthodox tradition as is theirs, and as spiritual. A mere wisp of wavering grace he seems, the very soul of that rhythm which sways his lovely comrades, wafting them this way, that way, to and fro, like puffs of swansdown.

In a ballet like this one hesitates to pick out any single feature for particular praise. But mention must be made of one small point which, in itself trivial, offers so excellent an example of the beautiful finish which Nijinsky carries even into the smallest details.

I refer to the exit at the end of his solo dance to the Mazurka. Do you remember how he doesn't simply walk or leap off into the wings, but stands quite still for a moment, and then, as if in answer to the summons of some attendant spirit, moves away, his face all glowing with the ecstasy of anticipation?

This always seems to me an inspired moment. And evidently it is by some such exquisite little touches that the Russians achieve that sense of imaginative conviction which so distinguishes their style.

THE BALLETS

This is a ballet quite different in type from those we have been considering. Its aim is essentially dramatic, and everything about it is designed to lead up to a single and thrilling climax. From the first brazen flourish of the overture one is aware that dread and terrible things are going to happen—though it is also this very music of the overture that gives the romantic touch to an atmosphere which would be otherwise almost unbearable.

"The scene," to quote for once from the official programme, "is the harem of Shahriar's palace. The fairest and best-beloved of his wives crouches by the monarch's side, and to engage his thoughts the chief eunuch summons before him three odalisques, who dance languorously. But Shahriar's mood is sinister, and he refuses to be diverted. For by his side is his younger brother, who has hinted the likelihood of infidelity and wickedness in his household. The brother has suggested their departure on a make-believe hunting party, to be followed by an unexpected return to the harem. Shahriar will try the brother's plan. He calls for armour and weapons, and the two royal brothers ceremoniously depart. The sound of the hunting-horns dies away. The women listen ; the coast is clear ; and they now assail the chief eunuch in an excited, fluttering crowd. He, doubting and fearing, yields to their demands ; and with the great keys at his belt opens the doors in the wall, whence emerge, some in copper and some in silver garb, a band of negro slaves, the harem-ladies' secret lovers. From the central door comes, clad in cloth of gold, the dark youth

Schererazade

who is the favourite of the queen herself."

This is Nijinsky, and from the moment of his entrance the drama takes on to itself a new and terrible meaning. The dark youth flickers here and there among the mazy crowd of slaves, hungry for the faithless wife of the sultan—she whose flesh also is parched and dry for the touch of his. He finds her soon, and his lecherous hands play over and over her body with a purpose too subtle, it seems, to take and hold her once and for all. And presently he leaves her, threading his way in and out of the passionate dancers, to lie at last on a soft cushion, like a flame of lust that smoulders and sinks but never dies. Now he has joined the orgy again. See him leap in the air, no man but a devil, the foul and heady essence that can spur these bodies of men and women to forget that they are human, and to lose themselves horribly in the last and frenzied abandonment of desire. Round him and around they swirl and swarm like drunken bees. Thank God ! you say, when suddenly the circle dissipates, disintegrates before your eyes, and it is the hour of judgment.

Seen for the first time, *Scheherazade* is one of the most startling of the ballets. The effect of the decoration, the costumes, the music, is intensely moving, while the dancing is only another instance of that wonderful flexibility of style which renders the Russian ballet so perfect an instrument for the expression of almost every phase of feeling. But on a second visit, or a third, this fine effect seems hardly maintained. Individual factors in the production, like the dancing of Nijinsky and the music, keep of course

their virtue ; but as a whole the drama
wears a little thin, and one becomes un-
easily conscious of the ugliness that lies
—it cannot be gainsayed — beneath the
splendour and the glitter.

Scheherazade, like the less important
ballet of *Thamar*, is concerned, you see,
to present a conventionally romantic
picture of oriental sensuality. Now, this
is a very legitimate thing to do. But
whereas *Thamar* is content to handle the
theme in a wholly simple and unmoral
manner, *Scheherazade* includes a deliberate
appeal to the human sense of shame
which, however good as morality, is surely
bad as art. For the sense of shame is not
compatible with æsthetic satisfaction, nor
do I think that its excitement, in a work
of art, would be enjoyed by a society
more delicate-minded than our own.

NIJINSKY

The miraculous automaton has often been used as a subject for drama, and long before the Russians came, Adeline Genée had captivated London with the doll-ballet of *Coppélia*. Such a theme must certainly be attractive to any dancer who has once mastered the free and graceful rhythms of natural life, inviting as it does to the control and exercise of a whole new range of attitude and movement. From the spectator's point of view there is also an amusing element of the bizarre in every such production, for it is almost as curious to watch a human being pretend to be a machine as it is to see a machine pretending to be human. So, at any rate, was the case in *Coppélia*.

But in this ballet of *Pétrouchka* the

interest is more subtle. The authors have delved deep, essaying to reveal as it were the very psychology of the inanimate, and to suggest some kind of soul life as existing in the bodies of mere marionettes. So, all those scenes which take place in the big box-like rooms behind the showman's tent, where the dolls are put away, are marked by an atmosphere of emotion as poignant as it is unreal. And they are full, too, of a strange subhuman beauty.

Now, it is Nijinsky's part to portray the dead mechanism of a doll, quickened to feverish life by jealousy. The beautiful lady-doll, you see, has bestowed her favours on a lusty blackamoor. What then can poor Pétrouchka do ? He is weak, a sort of puppet Pierrot. So there's nothing left for him but to try and emulate his rival's fascination. And this

he does in a dance whose frenzied pathos
supplies, oddly enough, the most purely
human touch in the entire Russian repertoire. It is Nijinsky's chance, and he
makes the most of it. For the rest of
the mimic drama is largely independent
of his genius. Which reminds one of the
fact that although nobody can dominate
a scene like Nijinsky, he is capable at
the same time of the most exquisite self-
restraint. Thus his Pétrouchka is never
out of the picture by the least breadth
of a hair ; and if there were any need
to accord individual honours they would
fall perhaps as reasonably to Karsavina,
for her lovely horn-dance is one of the
most memorable things in this ballet.

Pétrouchka, however, from beginning
to end, is full of a beauty as surprising
as it is diverse. We have a matchless
scene of pure pantomimic acting. The

musical setting has won the praise of those most qualified to form opinion, while the theme of the ballet is one which offers unusual stimulus to the imagination and intellectual sympathy of the audience. Judged as a complete whole, *Pétrouchka* still seems to me a little disappointing. Here and there the convention is overstrained, and one is often brought up too sharply by that danger which must always be lurking when the same method of pantomimic representation is applied to characters both human and non-human. The dolls by themselves behave most properly. And the crowd of Russian peasants by itself is quite convincing. But when the two kinds mingle together the effect becomes unsatisfying. For the essential difference between either mode of being is not sufficiently pronounced—cannot be, by the very convention of pantomime. And this is especially unfortunate when, as here, the whole meaning of the drama is bound up with the integrity of this differentiation.

But, after all, one is inclined to forget such shortcomings if only for the sake of that wonderful episode at the end, where slain Pétrouchka's spirit leans starkly over the wooden parapet of the booth, and sends the wretched showman gibbering off in horror, a tragic and unforgettable embodiment of the ghost of a doll.

PRÉLUDE À L'APRÈS-MIDI D'UN FAUNE

London has lately witnessed several attempts, more or less successful, at rendering the Greek spirit on the stage. There have been, for instance, performances of Prof. Murray's translations of *Euripides*, with a chorus trained in odd attitudes by Miss Margaret Morris. It would seem that the aim has been, in these choruses, to copy exactly images from the antique, images of woe, with long despairing arms and a monotonous faculty of lamentation borrowed from Ireland. Now and then we have caught at a gesture and exclaimed, "That's very like!" till the moment has passed, and we have seen only a woman, scantily clothed, and in a strange posture.

In spite of good intent, this mode of production has failed on the visual side, for the reason, no doubt, that models taken from the two-dimensional surface of old vases and bas-reliefs were transferred wholesale to a three-dimensional stage, thus abandoning the plastic convention which, on urn or frieze, was so beautifully adapted to the effect desired. Some dances of Isadora Duncan showed a truer feeling for just how much of the Grecian plastic manner could be rightly transferred from the flat to the round. But on a large scale it has been left for Nijinsky to imagine a classic scene which is equally vital in feeling and true to the tradition on which it is founded.

I am quite aware that the actual process of change from one attitude to another has in this ballet been the subject of criticism. The Greek convention, it is said, was such as to *suggest* movement ; and to make use of it in actual combination with movement is an artistic solecism. Better a series of static scenes or tableaux than this hybrid lapse from one static pose into another. Such argument, however, appears to be a little on the danger side of the pedantic, if only because the idea behind this ballet is

Le Faune

expressed in it so clearly, so forcibly, so
inevitably, that no other method than
this, one feels, would do. For here is
the very spirit of faun life, presented not
at all as the Greeks presented it, but as a
Greek might surely have rejoiced to see
it represented had he been born again
to-day.[1]

Now, Mr. Maurice Hewlett, who
knows more than most of us about the
psychology of fauns and fairies, has explored the difference between the human
kind and the fairy in words which are
beautifully relevant to the subject-matter
of this *Prélude*. " A comparison of the
fairy kind," he writes, " with human beings
is never successful, because into our images
of human beings we always impart self-

---

[1] I must interpolate here a word of admiration for the
beautiful scenery of M. Bakst, which so cunningly
supplies the needed link between Nijinsky's Greek attitudes and Debussy's very modern music.

consciousness. They know what they are doing. Fairies do not. . . . Human creatures, I think, know what they are doing only too well, because performance never agrees with desire. But with fairies, desire to do and performance are instinctive and simultaneous. If they think, they think in action, and in this they are far more like animals than human creatures."

How well Nijinsky has realised some such conception will be plain to anyone who has seen the *Prélude*. For quite apart from the beauty and the interest of the thing as a spectacle, his impersonation of a being so like us in the unspoken motives of its nature, so different in the instant activities of its life, is, to say the least of it, an astonishing achievement. This, indeed, is not simply ballet-dancing in a new mode. It is acting, and as subtle a piece of acting as has ever graced the stage of a theatre. For Nijinsky's is undoubtedly the faun of the poet's imagination: a type of the primal force of nature, and of the lusty instinct which is the fount of life.

JEUX

It's after dinner, in summer time, in the garden—such a quaint old garden, with little flower-beds set about like cheques on a board. It is very quiet in the garden, with that midsummer quiet that is half music, half silence. Perhaps we shall hear nightingales.

But no. To-night there's another kind of music—*Ping*, *pang*, *twong*—the music of the to-and-fro of tennis balls. Those lively young people must be playing up on the lawn by the Château—you know the game—the kind you play with red rackets and balls as big as melons. And actually here one comes ! A great white india-rubber thing, bouncing heavily over the hedge there. It's out of bounds, and they are sure to come to look for it soon, disturbing the solitude. Yes, I thought so. For here is our young friend, in the white flannels and the scarlet tie. What a jump ! He's down the bank like a streak of lightning ! But an instant too late. For the big white ball has eluded him, and off he goes, by the other path, very much on the wrong scent.

And now, what's this ? Why, I do believe it's the young man's playfellows coming to help him find the ball. They must have chosen the easy way through the shrubbery. Here they are, anyway, tripping into the garden, happily, prettily, all in white, with their short white skirts and stockings, and their white tennis shoes and white, tight jerseys. They are enjoying themselves, *ça se voit*. It was such fun playing tennis by moonlight, and really, you know, this is quite a little adventure, coming down into the mysterious flower-garden after ten o'clock, all alone, to look for a lost ball. . . .

For a while they search and search away among the flower-beds—but find nothing. And after all, what does it matter ? There are plenty of other balls in that cardboard box under the hammock on the lawn. Besides, the moon's so wonderfully bright to-night, and it makes one feel so queer, not like a real person at all, more like a nymph, or a fairy, or a sort of doll, or . . . But what was that ? Only Scarlet-tie. He too has evidently given up the search ; thinking, I suppose, that there are things far better worth the looking for, on a night like this, than a silly old india-rubber ball.

So he stands for a moment, watching the two girls. Then this way, that way, he begins to dance about among the flower-beds. This way, that way, the girls dance too, now chased, now chasing, now chased again. Look, he has caught her at last. No, it's the other one. And what need to be coy at long past ten o'clock of a moonlight night in a garden ?

Yet it's not for her alone that the moon's at the full to-night. Her friend, I can't believe that she came out into the garden just to play gooseberry ? For a moment, indeed, it looks like a case of *Two's company ;* but Scarlet-tie is a good fellow, he means to play the game, and knows, besides, that a proverb like

72

that could have been invented by none but the veriest amateur in flirtation.

Still, *amitié à trois*, even on a moonlight night, is a risky business. So easily over the border line it slips from jest to earnest. Scarlet-tie, it seems, has gone too far ; and now there are frowns, stampings of white tennis shoes, averted eyes. But he didn't mean it. Oh no. It was nothing but fun, you see. Won't they kiss and be friends ?

So *that's* all right, and "Come for a romp," cries Scarlet-tie. " I'll cut you a caper ! " And they fall to the dance again, leaping and dancing over and in and out of the flower-beds. Till at last, heated and breathless, they sink, the three of them, silently to the ground. A dear and curly head is pillowed trustingly on each of Scarlet-tie's broad shoulders. So comfy, they might have lain there for ever. . . .

But all at once, out of nowhere, flop ! A great white ball comes bounding and bouncing into the midst of them. They jump up, frightened, suddenly self-conscious. What was it ? Something— someone ?

Well, obviously there's only one thing to do now. And before you can count three, the garden is empty.

Only the big white india-rubber ball rolls lazily back down stage to settle itself somewhere, at last, among the footlights.

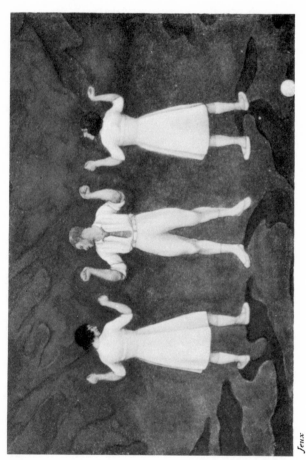

Jeux

CHAPTER V

THE NEW PHASE

In art, as in almost every sphere of human life, a deadly war is waged by each successive generation round the traditional legacies of its predecessor. In this warfare the odds are always heavily in favour of the assailant. Only that tradition which carries the seed of young vitality can persist. For it is obvious that tradition needs for its complete process not only the faculty of *handing down*, but also the grace of *being received*, so that we may almost take it as an axiom that the worth of any tradition is nicely proportionate to its ability to attract the allegiance, or at least the active interest, of the most important individuals of the new generation.

Oddly enough, the said important individuals are often just those who apparently owe least to what has gone before. The humdrum student follows his teacher with all the reverence that is fit. But your dominant force is always something of an anarchist. Whence arises that disrepute in which tradition is held by the *coteries*, who are usually too prone to be led away by the false glamour of appearance or their own conceit.

As a matter of fact, if a novel work of art possesses any qualities of real virtue, tradition, we may be sure, is at the bottom of it. For tradition can act very subtly, so subtly that its influence may long remain undetected, and then at last be only generally perceived through the revealing perspective of time. This is the·

reason why the mere layman is always ready to be surprised at strangeness, whereas the professional, who can detect the ever-exquisite relation of effect and cause, is seldom astonished, never long at a loss.

In the sphere of science, for instance, the sudden discovery of an X-ray, or the first flight of an aeroplane, sends a thrill of wonder through every honest reader of his morning's newspaper. But do you think that the man behind the scenes is so easily moved ? Of course not. For to him the discovery is a triumph perhaps, but not an unexpected triumph, and never anything more marvellous than the success which crowns a long series of experiments, begun and continued, or naturally evolving to a particular end. And in art it is just the same.

Take such a movement as that which

is now loosely but conveniently known as Post-Impressionism. Here is a thing which has proved sufficiently puzzling to the ordinary man. He cannot place it, cannot understand it at all. At first he laughs. Then maybe frowns. Till at length, obliged at any rate to go through the semblance of making up his mind, he brands the whole affair as perverse, ridiculous, the product of minds that have lost their bearings, and are wandering witless and rudderless on uncharted seas. And yet to those who are accustomed to a more critical view of painting, this same Post-Impressionism offers no such difficulties. Whether they approve of it or disapprove, they are not deceived into mistaking it for a monster. For however shocking at the first glance, it quickly becomes evident to their perception as a genuine movement whose antecedents are clearly traceable through Manet to Ingres and the whole régime of the classical art of France.

Truth is that there's no such thing as a complete novelty either in life or in the arts. Novelty may, indeed, be sought after ; but if it is attained, it is only as an intellectual freak (like Futurism), not as an instance of organic growth. And growth is all that matters. And for growth, tradition in some form or other is the first essential. For tradition, you see, is only another name for that principle of continuity without which the very idea of growth—let alone progress—is impossible.

Now, the right functioning of tradition has never, perhaps, been more perfectly exemplified than in the case of the Russian Ballet which, greeted here on its first appearance as something absolutely

new, soon transpired to be the culmination
of a long development which linked together in one long process the most seem-
ingly extravagant novelties with the beginnings of modern ballet in the eighteenth
century. I have already tried to suggest
the main steps in this development up to
the time of M. Fokine's supremacy as
producer to the Diaghilew ballet. It remains to chronicle the sudden side-track
which the ballet has taken since then
as exemplified in the three new ballets
for which Nijinsky is directly responsible:
L'Après-Midi d'un Faune, *Jeux*, and *Le
Sacre du Printemps*.

Consider the repertoire of the Russian
Ballet as it existed previously to the first
production of *Faune* in the autumn of
1912. Roughly, the ballets then in performance might be divided into three
groups—the epic, the atmospheric, and

the dramatic. In groups 1 and 2 we had ballets like *Le Pavillon d'Armide*, *Le Carnaval*, *Les Sylphides*, *Le Spectre de la Rose*; in group 3, ballets like *Scheherazade*, *Cléopatre*, and *Thamar*, all of which showed a definite trend towards dramatic emphasis as well as a preoccupation with that sort of agonised sensuality which one associates with the German and somewhat hectic imagination of Prof. Reinhardt. Some of M. Fokine's finest creations were the result of this influence, yet it was soon clear that in the long run dramatic intensity could only be maintained at the expense of a weakening in the choreographic interest; and such weakening in fact was very noticeable in *Thamar*, and still more so in the later ballet of *Le Dieu Bleu*. There were people, in fact, who began to be suspicious of further development on these lines, fearing that it would prove harmful to the pure spirit of Russian dancing. And, after all, in any ballet the dance is the thing, so that an influence which tends to obliterate its essential importance is naturally to be deplored. Nevertheless, for a time, the pantomimic tendency seemed to offer the only possible path of progress, and that a new outlet was found for the ballet on legitimately choreographic lines, must be laid very largely to the credit of Nijinsky.

Let us, though, guard against the mistaken belief that the new idea came bubbling out of Nijinsky's mind entirely unrelated to what was being thought and done by his contemporaries. This new phase of ballet-dancing, for all its power to shock or amuse a certain section of the public, here and in Paris, is no isolated venture standing by itself and destined to solitary success or lonely failure. Rather is it an instance of a widespread tendency which has been manifest of late in almost every department of art—a tendency of reaction against the complex achievement of a self-conscious age. For without implying that Nijinsky's art is derived in any essential respect from Post-Impressionism, it is yet not irrelevant to record the fact of Nijinsky's ardent admiration for the work of Paul Gauguin, or to mention the undoubted influence of the same master upon the style of stage-setting adopted in *Jeux* and *Le Sacre du Printemps*.

But even more noticeably than the new school of painting has that of music been a source of inspiration to Nijinsky, and in this connection two composers, Claude Debussy and Igor Stravinsky, stand out for special reference. Of the two, Stravinsky, the young Russian, was first in the field, his relation with the Russian Ballet dating from the period of *l'Oiseau de Feu*, an old-fashioned fairy-tale ballet, endowed with an exotic air, however, by reason of its very modern musical setting. In this music was the germ of a new attitude towards the ballet, a germ which in *Pétrouchka* began actually to bear fruit. For sheer pantomime as much of it was, *Pétrouchka* showed, here and there, a most significant reliance on purely choreographic gesture—a reliance which was only made possible by certain definite qualities in the musical accompaniment.

What these qualities were it may be hard to indicate, but anyone who has heard the music will remember its vivid intimacy of feeling, its freedom from formality, its utter abandonment of the conventional means of climax. Stravinsky makes no attempt to strike the hearer into an atti-

84

Pétrouchka

tude of surprise. His most daring effects
are introduced quite informally and by
the way (*e.g.* the barrel-organ in *Pétrouchka*), and there is always a complete
absence from his style of musical rhetoric.
So his music achieves its purpose almost
unawares, insinuates itself into your attention rather than commands it, and relies
for its effect on severity of simplifica-
tion and on a sort of winning trustful-
ness that the meaning of the work is
sufficiently interesting to dispense with
the trappings of sentiment or artificial
thrill.

Just this might be said with equal
truth of Nijinsky's choreographic inno-
vations which have shown us dancing
stripped of its conventional attributes, a
thing of accent rather than of rhythm,
and almost destitute of grace, though still
dancing essentially, as opposed to panto-

mime. For pantomime, remember, seeks to express emotion through realistic gestures, whereas dancing makes use of a convention of its own — a gesture in which the ordinary values of realism have no place.

The apparent oddness of a ballet like *Jeux* is due, then, not at all to perversity of subject, but to the employment of a dance-convention with which we do not happen to have been familiar. The *Faune*, you see, was played in London without protest and was quickly one of the most appreciated of Russian ballets, largely because the convention employed in it, though new to the stage, was familiar enough to anyone who could boast of a smattering of Greek culture. But in *Jeux*, where a more novel convention was practised on a modern theme, the stalls gracefully tittered and the critics next morning wanted to know what it was all about ; while even those who had got so far as to discover that much were almost unanimous in voting the whole concern amusing, perhaps, but really too trivial to be worthy of serious attention.

From one point of view the theme of *Jeux* certainly is trivial. Expressed in terms of pantomime it might easily have seemed little more than a thing of merely fascinating commonplace, like a scene out of some musical comedy played in dumb show. But here Nijinsky comes in, and raises it all to a higher power of meaning by the sincerity of his purpose and by his use of a convention which so combines a sense of character with an austere impersonality of action, that it can turn a particular piece of fact or fancy into an instance of universal truth. For *Jeux* is something more than a scene of charming dalliance between a young man and two young girls. It is flirtation in the abstract, the essence of delightful adolescence, clothed in the garments of to-day, but equally true of yesterday, to-morrow, or the day after.

For all its exquisiteness, there is in *Jeux*, however, a certain experimental feeling which marks it still as the work of a period of transition. Now and then Nijinsky seems to relapse into a pose that is derived from an earlier convention, and once or twice we find a repetition of attitude which the action does not require. It is lucky for our present purpose that there is yet another production which shows Nijinsky's method in its fullest power, exercised without restraint or hesitancy and upon a theme exactly suited to its peculiar manner.

Le Sacre du Printemps raises so many

questions, artistic and otherwise, that it might well form the subject of a whole book. It demands to be treated as carefully from the standpoint of archæology as of art, and even the theologian might find a good deal to say about it from his own particular point of view.

At a first visit it appeared to be not much more than an exhibition of antic savagery, a marshalling of broad splashes of colour, a monotonous variation on the theme of centric and eccentric circularities. But over all, in spite of much that seemed absurd, one felt the presence of a guiding intelligence, ordering all things to an end that was not yet clear, but, even in obscurity, beautiful. On a second visit, however, when one could forget to be amused, the whole spectacle gathered to itself a coherence and significance which proved its purely visual charm to be, in the truest sense, expressive of a fine idea.

With the simple directness of great art *Le Sacre du Printemps* points the imagination not away to an imaginary world of sentiment or ideal emotion, but back to the real but misty past of human life, to a time when man was still at hostile grips with nature, when the struggle between rich and poor had not begun, but when rich and poor alike were ranged together in a common strife with the cruelty of winds and waters. It was the life of the herd, and if we have ever glibly used or read the phrase "herd instinct" without realising what it meant, here it is, realised before our very eyes.

Primarily, we have said, this early life of man was a life of fear; but also it was a life of ecstasy and, now and then, of a strange communion with nature such as we of to-day can never know. For not always was nature unkind. At certain times and seasons, how, why, man knew not, she would take to herself the aspect of a most kindly goddess, and then would man feel himself to be so near to her and so grateful that nothing it seemed could be too great or too fearful a sacrifice if only he might attain again to that delight. And it was found that the favour of the goddess could indeed be gained, were she propitiated with fitting rites, so that after cruellest winter, from every shoot and tendril the sap would rise, and the brown earth bring forth its secrets, and man once more be warm, and the children play in the sun.

This is the holy rite of prayer and sacrifice which is celebrated in *Le Sacre du Printemps*. There is no other plot, and we need only sit and watch with a kind of grim but simple wonder the gradual completion of the ceremony.

On a luminous spring evening the young men of the tribe are being instructed in the appointed incantations. Soon a bevy of girls approach, and we have an episode of simulated rape, the ritual act which is the symbol of the clan's desire for fruitfulness, for sturdy sons and daughters to carry on its life, and to assure the safety in old age of those now at their prime. Then, huddled together in little fumbling groups, these strange worshippers begin to pay their homage to the powers of the earth and of the stars. To a weird music they perform what is due, to a rhythm of unwearying persistence that throbs through all the festival, so that at last the whole broad earth seems to be throbbing, throbbing to the beat of it.

THE NEW PHASE

But this is not all. The conscience of the tribe demands the sacrifice of its fairest flower, to the end that all the rest may live on and enjoy the blessings of security and a pious heart. A young girl, the chosen of her fellows, is to be sanctified by acting out to the bitter end this drama of propitiation. Men of the tribe, clothed in the likeness of bears, flock around to witness the sacrifice, and the chosen maiden herself stands forth and resigns herself to the frenzied movements of the dance that celebrates at once her death and her apotheosis. This dance betrays the pitiful but haunting hope of primitive man, bound by chains as he lies, the slave to his own fear. For the limbs of the dancer seem fettered by hands unseen, so that at the moment when freedom is almost won, they relapse once more into bondage, helplessly jerking out their life in a divine paralysis. And now at last the sacrifice is accomplished. In dreadful travesty of death the girl languishes to the ground, and the bear-skinned tribesmen gather round to carry her away to burial, shoulder high.

Such is the ballet of *Le Sacre du Printemps*, if ballet it can be called. And however much you may dislike it, you cannot deny its interest as an attempt to track the art of dancing to its source in the rituals of savagery. Whatever its æsthetic value, this aspect of the thing at least is of importance. For its aim is altogether serious, and I have it from Nijinsky himself that the whole spectacle has been designed with the most reverent reliance on existing records of Muscovite life in the fourth century before Christ.

But if archæological accuracy were the

only merit of *Le Sacre du Printemps* its claim to attention would indeed be limited. It displays, however, technical features of no inferior interest, some of which are also of first-class importance in the evolution of the ballet.

Hitherto, swiftness and lightness have been regarded as prime necessities in the modern ballet. The ability of dancers has been estimated according to their excellence in these respects, and the more the eyes of the spectators have been dazzled the more, it would seem, have they been pleased. *Jeux* and the *Faune* both showed that there were other possibilities in the dance, and now *Le Sacre du Printemps* conclusively contradicts all old ideas as to the importance of those qualities which were previously held to be essential.

For such movement as there is in this

ballet is deliberate in the extreme. The
attitudes of the dancers evolve with the
measured inevitability of a slowly-turned
kaleidoscope, and as for lightness—the
whole performance is a studied demonstra-
tion of the attractive force of the earth
and of the triumph of gravity. I have
heard that if we were transported all at
once to a planet like Jupiter, much greater
in bulk than our earth, the sense of bodily
weight would be so increased that we
should find it difficult to walk upright.
Such apparently is the feeling of the
people in *Le Sacre du Printemps*. The
earth seems like an enormous magnet
which continually drags them down-
wards to itself, and such leapings as
they do from time to time indulge in
cannot result from any aspiring liveli-
ness of spirit, but are traceable, more
probably, to their wish to encourage, by

such well-known acts of primitive ritual, the growth of crops and herbs.

However unorthodox in its effect, the manner in which *Le Sacre du Printemps* was designed was the same as that laid down by the regular tradition of the ballet. First the music was composed, and then the dances, though previous consultation between composer and choreographer had fixed the main lines on which the ballet was to proceed. This must account for the fusion, not only apparent but real, between the dances arranged by Nijinsky and Stravinsky's score. I doubt, indeed, if this music would prove effective in the concert hall, but its inseparable connection with the ballet must be accounted a virtue rather than an evidence of limitation.

To audiences accustomed to the graceful idealism of former productions, *Le Sacre du Printemps* came, as we have said, with something of a surprise. Almost every quality of beauty or dramatic interest which we had grown to expect in a ballet was absent from this one, and the first impression of many was that the whole thing was little more than a piece of uncouth and impudent mockery.

Yet if only one can bring oneself to view this very uncouthness as part of a large design, not simply as its dominating feature, one will have come a long way towards appreciating the ballet in the spirit intended by its creator. For besides the uncouthness of *Le Sacre du Printemps*, how much there is in it of beauty and deep emotion ! Religion, the thing that binds and has tortured and nerved mankind throughout the ages, is still with us to-day, and there is nothing alien from modern thought or interest in this presentment of its early manifestation. For the sake of such a theme one can surely spare a little of that gracefulness which in other Russian ballets is lavished so generously.

As for the theme itself, we may admit that it is a strange and novel one, and that by making use of it Nijinsky seems to be claiming that a fresh range of subject should be opened up, or rather reopened, for the dance. But this implies, not a destruction of what has been valued in the past and will go on being valuable, but a gradual evolution towards a new expressiveness and a new technique. Strange things are bound to happen. Yet if reason and courage are behind them, why should we be afraid? Prettiness is very well in its way, but life is greater, and truth greater still. And in this truth— this reality which is the gleam that for ever eludes us—lies, as some believe, the hope of truest beauty.

This, at any rate, is the hope of Nijinsky. And for this he will labour while he may—for, in his own brave words, " *La Grace, le Charme, le Joli sont rangés tout autour du point central qu'est le Beau. C'est pour le Beau que je travaille.*"

CHAPTER VI

CONCLUSION

THE praise which the Russian Ballet has almost universally received in England seems to offer one of the rare instances of our ability to appreciate a good thing when we see it. On that we may congratulate ourselves. But I am reminded that this appreciation is by no means universal, and that in Russia itself there is a section of opinion to whom the later developments of the Diaghilew ballet are frankly abhorrent.

Hitherto, we must remember, the ballet in Russia has been an exclusively aristocratic form of art. It has relied for its existence on State patronage, and has inevitably preserved the bias of all things royal towards the conventional and the correct. But now that private enterprise has furnished an independent outlet, the ballet has become a splendid playground for that personal and adventurous spirit which is the first result of emancipation. This, of course, means many enemies in the country of its origin, and explains the fact that, like so many achievements of the modern Russian spirit, the new art of Russian dancing is an art of exiles.

In this country, however, the Russian Ballet has had to face no active hostility, and a recent pronouncement of Mr. Gordon Craig affords, I think, the only serious and public criticism of its principles.

Briefly, his complaint is that the appeal

of the ballet is too material—the beauty of individual human bodies acting upon our senses, stimulating a physical appreciation which excludes the serene spiritual revelation that is the aim of art.

If anyone has a right to make such a stricture it is Mr. Craig; and however little we may be disposed to take his point of view, it may at least remind us that there are worlds of feeling which the Russians have still to conquer, and that Nijinsky himself, though, indeed, he has shown us something of the dance under its first ritual inspiration, has as yet done nothing to restore to it that social significance which was once the secret of its appeal.

That for the Future. In the meantime, we may be well content. The memory of a hundred wonderful nights is enough.   And if Nijinsky never danced again we should know that his fame would be safe—the fame of one who, more perhaps than any man living, has made beauty for his generation.

TABLE OF BALLETS

TABLE OF BALLETS PERFORMED IN LONDON IN WHICH NIJINSKY HAS APPEARED

Title of Ballet	Inventor of the Dances	Designer of Scenery and Costumes	Composer of Music
Giselle	Corali	Benois	Adams
Le Lac des Cygnes	Petipa	Korovin and Golovin	Tschaikovsky
Aurore et le Prince. (*Pas de Deux* from La Belle au Bois Dormant)	Petipa	—	Tschaikovsky
Le Pavillon d'Armide	Fokine	Benois	Tcherepnin
Narcisse	Fokine	Bakst	Tcherepnin
Le Spectre de la Rose	Fokine	Bakst	Weber
Les Sylphides	Fokine	Bakst	Chopin
Le Carnaval	Fokine	Bakst	Robert Schumann
Scheherazade	Fokine	Bakst	Rimsky-Korsakov
Cléopatre	Fokine	Bakst	Arensky
Le Dieu Bleu	Fokine	Bakst	Reynaldo Hahn
Pétrouchka	Fokine	Benois	Stravinsky
Prélude à l'Après-Midi d'un Faune	Nijinsky	Bakst	Debussy
Jeux	Nijinsky	Bakst	Stravinsky

INDEX OF NAMES AND BALLETS

109

NIJINSKY